Special thanks to Sue Mongredien

First published in 2010
by Faber and Faber Ltd
Bloomsbury House
74–77 Great Russell Street
London WC1B 3DA

Printed in England by Bookmarque, Croydon, UK

Series created by Working Partners Limited, London W6 0QT

A CIP record for this book
is available from the British Library

978–0–571–24806–3

2 4 6 8 10 9 7 5 3 1

The Big Parade

By Jessie Little

Illustrated by Penny Dann

ff

faber and faber

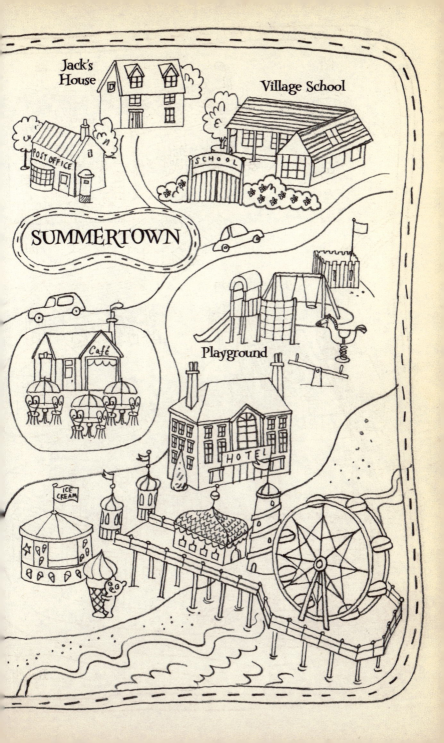

Chapter One

'Willow! Willow! Wake up!'

Seven-year-old Willow Thompson
opened a sleepy eye at the voice – then
jerked wide awake as she realised that Toby,
her cuddly blue Hoozle bear, was standing

by the pillow,
prodding her.
It was still
something of
a surprise that
he could come

to life and talk to her, but then again, this summer had been full of surprises so far!

'What's up?' she asked. 'Are you OK?'

'I'm too excited to stay in bed,' Toby replied, bouncing up and down. 'It's the Summertown Spectacular today!'

Willow sat up. Of course! She and Toby had been looking forward to this day ever since they'd come to stay with Auntie Suzy for the summer holidays. Summertown was the friendly seaside resort where Auntie Suzy lived above her toy shop, and every year, the whole town got together with a parade to celebrate everything that made Summertown such a special place to live.

'Are you ready for your starring role in the parade, then?' Willow asked, hugging Toby. 'Won't it be fun?'

The Hoozles were cuddly soft toys,

hand-made by Auntie Suzy and sold in the shop. This summer Willow had discovered something very special about the Hoozles – they were all alive, and could walk and talk, just like she did. They were such lovely friendly creatures, too! Well, most of them, anyway. It was a shame about Croc, the mean orange crocodile Hoozle, but the less said about him the better, in Willow's opinion.

Because the Hoozles were so well-loved in Summertown, the town's Mayor himself would be carrying Wizard, an owl-shaped Hoozle, on the first float of the parade. Auntie Suzy, Willow and her brother Freddie would walk in front, carrying the other Hoozles. It was just going to be so exciting!

Willow quickly put on her best summer

dress and ran along to the kitchen where Auntie Suzy was making breakfast. Freddie was there too with Wobbly, his lion Hoozle. He looked up eagerly as Willow came in. 'Look, I've combed Wobbly's mane especially,' he said, showing Willow. 'Doesn't he look smart?'

'He looks brilliant,' Willow agreed, then turned to her aunt. 'What time will the Mayor get here?'

Auntie Suzy glanced up at the big wall-

clock. 'Well, he should have been here
ten minutes ago actually,' she said with a
frown. 'I'm sure he's on his way, though.
Once he's picked up Wizard and we've
finished breakfast, we can make our way
down to the starting line with the other
Hoozles.' She peered out of the window.
'It's stopped raining, thank goodness. It was
pouring all night so let's hope it stays dry
today.'

While Auntie Suzy put some toast on,
Willow decided to pop down to the toy
shop with Toby. She wanted to wish Wizard
luck in private before he was whisked away
by the Mayor.

'Back in a minute,' she called, hurrying
downstairs. Three Hoozles lived in the
shop, and they were known as the Hoozle
Council. There was Wizard, of course, who

was the first Hoozle Suzy had ever made and the group leader. Then there was Lovely, a pink and purple pony Hoozle, who'd once belonged to Willow's mum, and finally, Grouchy, a cute penguin Hoozle.

'Hi, guys,' Willow said softly as she pushed open the shop door. 'Are you all OK?'

The Hoozles were up on their shelf as usual and they all turned towards her as she came in. 'Where is he?' Wizard burst out anxiously. 'He's never usually late.'

Willow blinked in surprise. 'Um . . . Auntie Suzy said she thinks he must be on his way,' she replied.

'He should have been here ages ago,' Grouchy grumbled. 'What's keeping him?'

'I don't know,' Willow said. 'I'm sure he'll be here soon, though.'

'Maybe we should go and look for him?' Toby suggested.

'Yes, do,' Lovely urged, tossing her mane out of her eyes. She stamped a foot impatiently. 'Come on, Mr Mayor! Hurry up!'

Willow ran back upstairs. 'Shall I nip to the Mayor's house?'

she asked, gobbling her toast quickly. 'It's only down the road, isn't it? Just in case he's forgotten or something.'

'Would you mind? That would be really

helpful,' Auntie Suzy replied. 'If he's running late, just tell him I'll meet him – and you – at the start of the parade. I'll keep the Hoozles with me in case he's already on his way.'

As soon as Willow had finished her breakfast and brushed her teeth, she put Toby into her backpack with his head peeping out, and set off for the Mayor's house.

It didn't take them long to walk along the sea front and up the road where he lived. The pavement was filled with puddles from the heavy rain the night before, and the Mayor's garden looked positively squelchy with mud as Willow made her way along the front path. She knocked on his door and waited. Nothing happened.

She knocked again, louder this time, but

the house remained quiet. 'Looks like he's already left,' she said to Toby after a few seconds. 'He must have gone to Auntie Suzy's a different way, and we've missed him.'

'I'm not so sure,' Toby said from where he was in the backpack. 'Look what's on that holly bush by the door, there. Orange fluff!'

Willow saw where Toby was pointing, and her heart sank. It was a shade of orange that she recognised straight away . . . exactly the same as Croc's fur. 'Oh no,' she said. 'If Croc's been here, that only means one thing – trouble!'

Chapter Two

'What's he up to now, I wonder?' Willow muttered, glancing around. 'Do you think he's trying to spoil the parade?'

Toby shrugged his soft blue shoulders. 'Probably, knowing him,' he replied. 'Maybe he's lying in wait, so that he can kidnap Wizard?'

'We can't let that happen,' Willow said at once. 'Come on, let's see if we can find him.'

She and Toby looked all around the soggy front garden in search of Croc, or

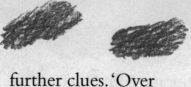

further clues. 'Over
here!' Toby hissed after a
few moments, and Willow
saw that he'd spotted some
large, man-sized muddy
footprints on the front path.

'These must be the Mayor's footprints,'
Willow said, feeling excited at the
discovery. 'So he's gone out, at least – but
did he get away before Croc could play
one of his horrid tricks?'

'Let's follow the footprints,' Toby
suggested. 'I know we haven't found Croc,
but I think it's more important to find the
Mayor first and make sure the parade goes
ahead, don't you?'

'I agree,' Willow said, picking him up and

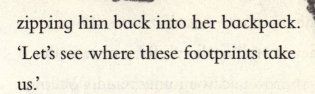

zipping him back into her backpack.
'Let's see where these footprints take
us.'

The muddy footprints led all
the way back to the sea front. 'His
shoes must have been really muddy,'
Willow commented, rather surprised.

'I know,' Toby whispered. 'I
thought the footprints were drying
up a moment ago, then they went
through another puddle and that
seemed to make them muddy again.
Lucky for us!'

The footprints rounded the
corner of the sea front, and then
stopped outside an ice-cream shop.
Willow stared. 'That's strange,' she

murmured. 'Why would he want an ice cream so early in the morning when he had the parade to get to?'

'They do sell tea and coffee as well in there,' sharp-eyed Toby whispered, noticing the sign in the window. 'Maybe that's why he came in?'

'Only one way to find out,' Willow said, and walked into the shop. 'Hi,' she said to the lady behind the counter. 'Has the

 Mayor been in today?'

'The Mayor? No,' the lady replied, shaking her head. 'I haven't seen him, and I've been here all morning.'

'Oh,' Willow said, feeling baffled.

Why would the Mayor come to the ice-cream shop and not go in, she wondered. It didn't make sense. 'Thanks anyway,' she remembered to say, wandering out again.

'I think we should go back to the toy shop to see if the Mayor's turned up there yet,' she said to Toby as she walked away.

She hadn't gone very far from the ice-cream shop, when all of a sudden, Croc popped out from an alleyway. 'Well, what do we have here?' he sneered. 'Goody Two-Shoes and her tiresome teddy! I should have known you two would be meddling . . . but guess what?

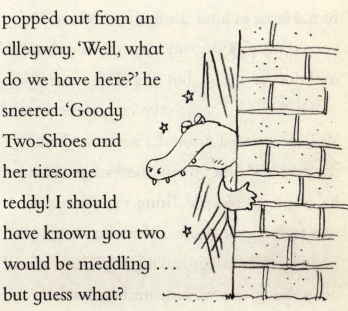

You're too late. The big parade won't be taking place today now.'

'What do you mean? What have you done?' Willow asked, rounding on him, but Croc merely laughed.

'Let's just say the Mayor's fate is sealed,' he said, his eyes glittering with mischief.

Croc said this so meaningfully, Willow could tell he was dropping some kind of hint. He must have plotted something to keep the Mayor away from the toy shop and the parade . . . but what?

'Hi, Willow!' came a voice just then and Willow whirled around. There was Jack, the boy she'd met a few weeks ago with his elephant Hoozle, Bouncer. Nice as it was to see Jack again, she really hoped he hadn't just seen her talking to Croc – after all, nobody else was meant to know the

Hoozles' secret. Willow's heart thumped uncomfortably. Had she just been found out?

Chapter Three

'Hi,' she said, swallowing hard and trying to appear normal. Jack was making Bouncer wave his arm to Toby, so Willow made Toby wave back, even though Toby could wave his arm perfectly well on his own of course. Phew, Jack hadn't noticed her talking to Croc, after all.

She quickly glanced down at where Croc had been standing but he'd vanished, thank goodness. 'How are you, Jack?' she asked, her heart slowing in relief.

'Good,' he said. 'Can't wait for the Summer Spectacular!' Then he looked puzzled. 'Wait – I thought you and your aunt were leading the parade,' he said. 'Shouldn't you be over there by now?'

'Well . . .' Willow began, not quite sure how to explain. 'Um . . . it's a kind of game,' she improvised after a moment. 'The Mayor's hidden somewhere and he's left a strange clue. I've got to find him before the parade goes ahead.'

'Wow,' Jack said. 'That sounds like fun. Can I help?'

Again, Willow hesitated. But maybe it was a good idea – two heads were better than one, weren't they? 'Sure,' she said. 'The clue is that the Mayor's fate is sealed. Any ideas?'

'The Mayor's fate is sealed,' Jack repeated, thinking hard. 'Well, it could mean that the Mayor is sealed up somewhere – as in locked in.' Locked in! It would be just like horrid Croc to trap the Mayor somewhere so that he couldn't take part in the parade.

'I bet you're right,' Willow said. 'Great thinking, Jack. Now all we need to do is find out where he's locked in.'

'Hmmm,' said Jack thoughtfully. 'Well, whenever I lose something, I go back to the last place I saw it,' he reasoned. 'So why don't we go back to the last place the Mayor was, then look for more clues.'

'Let's head back towards his house, then,' Willow said. 'Maybe Toby and I missed something when we were there.'

They started walking away from the seafront and back towards the Mayor's house. Willow was still carrying Toby and after a while, she decided to put him in her backpack again. She opened the bag and popped him in, then zipped a little way up to stop him falling out. Unfortunately, she pulled the zip a tiny bit too far and it caught Toby's furry neck.

'Oh! Sorry!' Willow gasped at once, yanking the zip back again. 'Are you OK?'

Toby didn't reply, and it took Willow a moment to realise why. Jack was staring at her as if she were mad and she blushed bright red. No wonder

Toby hadn't said anything – Jack was right there next to her. So much for keeping the Hoozle secret! she thought, feeling hot and flustered. She'd nearly given the game away completely! She faked a laugh. 'Just ignore me,' she said to Jack. 'I always talk to Toby. Anyway. Clues. Let's keep hunting for clues.'

Jack was still looking at her a bit oddly but Willow busied herself peering down at the ground, the nearby gardens, the

roadside – anything, in fact, other than Jack's face. They were nearing the Mayor's house again and Willow stiffened with excitement as she noticed another set of muddy footprints leading away from the house – this time in the direction of the town centre. She was sure they hadn't been there before. Had the Mayor come back to the house for something and gone out again?

'Look!' she cried, pointing at the pavement ahead. 'The Mayor's footprints!'

Jack looked puzzled. 'How can he be leaving footprints if he's locked in somewhere?' he asked.

Good question. Willow had been wondering the same thing. Maybe they were wrong about the Mayor being locked in? 'I don't know,' she confessed. 'But I really

think we should follow those footprints.
They're another clue, and with a bit of
luck, they'll lead us right to the Mayor!'

Chapter Four

Willow and Jack followed the footprint trail
along the high street. Flags and bunting
had been tied along the roadside, and lots
of shops had posters up advertising the
Summertown Spectacular. Balloons bobbed
and swayed where they'd been tied to
lampposts, and the road had been emptied
of all traffic. Everything was in place for
the parade to begin – apart from the
Mayor himself!

Willow hoped more than ever that they'd

be able to find him soon. There was less than an hour now before the parade was due to start. What had Croc done?

The footprints came to a sudden stop outside the Summertown bookshop. 'Oh,' said Jack, scratching his head. 'What now?'

'Let's go and ask if he's been in here,' Willow said, pushing open the shop door and walking in. 'Come on.'

She and Jack went up to the counter where a friendly-looking man was unpacking a huge box of colourful books. 'Can I help you?' he asked.

'We're looking for the Mayor,' Willow said politely. 'Has he been in here today?'

'Not today, no,' the man said. 'Sorry.'

'Thanks,' Willow said, trying to hide her disappointment.

A sales assistant staggered by with a

towering pile of books just then, and a
few picture books slid off the top and fell
to the floor, pages fluttering. 'Let me help,'
Jack said, passing Bouncer to Willow and
crouching down to gather them up.

Willow perched on a sofa near a display
cabinet as she waited for Jack, drumming

her fingers impatiently while he followed the sales assistant with the books. It was very nice of him to help but they didn't have time to hang around here! She needed to solve the mystery of the missing Mayor. It really was strange that his footprints had led them here, yet nobody had seen him – just like at the ice-cream shop earlier.

'Where can he be?' Toby cried, from where he was sitting on the back of the couch with Bouncer.

Bouncer twirled his soft velvety trunk. 'I'm getting worried,' he said, his voice low and rumbly.

But before Willow could speak, a blur of orange appeared from behind the couch. Croc! And his mouth was open in a toothy grin.

'Worried?' he taunted. 'So you should

be! Not long
till the parade
starts, after
all . . . but
oh dear, the
Mayor's a bit
tied up right
now!' He
chortled and

then narrowed his eyes at Bouncer. 'Ahh,'
he said. 'So there's a new kid in town.
Hasn't anyone warned you about me yet?'

And with that, he made a dive for
Bouncer. Willow knew exactly what Croc
was up to – he was trying to steal Bouncer's
pocket heart, just as he'd stolen Wobbly's.
Every Hoozle had a little pocket stitched
on to them, and their owner was asked
to put a special toy or thing inside the

pocket, which became the Hoozle's heart. The pocket heart was a symbol of the love between the child and their Hoozle, and without it, Hoozles felt very unwell. Luckily for Wobbly, Willow and Toby had managed to get his pocket heart back to him, but they knew that Croc couldn't be trusted.

'Get off him!' Willow hissed now, trying to stop Croc from attacking Bouncer. Toby, too, leaped in to protect the cuddly elephant and pushed Croc away. Unfortunately, as he shoved Croc, the

orange Hoozle fell backwards, knocking
a glass vase off the display cabinet behind
them.

Willow could hardly breathe with
fright – she was going to get in so much
trouble if that vase smashed! – but luckily,
quick-thinking
Bouncer lunged
for the vase and
just managed to
catch it in time.

'Well done,'
Willow said in
relief, taking
the vase and
standing it up again.

'Yeah, well caught, Bouncer,' she heard
Jack say, and turned to see him standing
there looking bewildered. 'Did that really

just happen?' he asked, his eyes wide and disbelieving. 'Did I really just see Bouncer moving?'

Willow nodded. 'Yes,' she said uncertainly. 'But humans aren't supposed to know, so—'

'Ha!' Croc interrupted with a sneer. 'I don't care how many stupid humans see me, I'm still stopping the soppy parade.' And before Willow could grab him, he'd darted away through a side door.

Jack was still looking completely stunned, but Willow knew she had to react fast. 'Come on, Jack,' she cried, grabbing Toby and running after Croc. 'Follow me!'

She rushed out of the side door, just in time to see Croc snatching up two sticks and pelting away with them. She stared, her mind whirring as she realised that the sticks had cardboard feet stuck to the bottom of

them. 'Hold on a minute,' she said to Jack.
'Those footprints we were following weren't
made by the Mayor after all. Croc must
have made them to fool us!'

'He must have dipped the cardboard feet
in mud and used them to print the trail,'
Jack realised. 'But why would he do such
a thing?' He rubbed his eyes. 'Willow, am I
in a really weird dream, or is this actually

happening?'

'It's happening,' Willow replied, as Croc dodged around a corner and disappeared from view. 'And now I'm more confused than ever.'

She sighed and Toby snuggled himself against her. 'Let's think about the clues again,' he said. 'The Mayor's locked in and "a bit tied up", according to Croc. We know now that those footprints were just a false trail made by Croc, to throw us off the scent. Which means . . .'

'Which means the Mayor might never have left his house!' Willow finished excitedly. 'Toby, you're a genius!'

Chapter Five

Willow and Jack rushed back towards the
Mayor's house and once they were there,
Willow knocked on the door as loudly as
she could. She also opened the letterbox
and shouted through it: 'Is anyone there?'

She put her ear to the letterbox as she
listened for a reply – and then she heard a
muffled voice. 'Help! Help me!'

Willow's heart skipped a beat. The voice
was male – it had to be the Mayor's! 'It's
him,' she said to Jack. 'He must be locked in

somewhere. How are we going to get him out?'

'There's a window open up there, look,' Bouncer said, pointing upwards with his trunk.

Jack almost jumped out of his skin at the sound of Bouncer's voice. 'You can talk as well?' he gaped, staring down at his Hoozle.

Bouncer winked one button eye. 'You bet,' he said. 'And you can hear me. Isn't it great?'

Meanwhile, Toby was staring up at the open window. 'Bouncer, I reckon you and I could squeeze through that gap,' he said thoughtfully. 'If we can just get up there ...'

'Jack could throw us,' Bouncer put in. 'I've seen him with a cricket ball and he's a mean shot!'

Jack grinned. 'Thanks,' he said.

'Willow's a good
shot too,' Toby said
loyally. 'You could
throw me all the
way up to that
window, couldn't
you?'

Willow gazed
from Toby to the
window. 'I'll give
it a go,' she said.
'One, two, three . . .
Hoozles away!' She
hurled Toby up as
high as she could,
almost scared to
watch as he soared
into the air. She
hoped he wouldn't

bash against the wall of the house, or worse, crash down hard on the ground.

But her aim was perfect, and Toby landed neatly on the windowsill. He got to his feet and waved down at them.

'Now it's your turn, Bouncer,' Jack said. 'Ready? Here we go!'

He too threw his Hoozle up into the air. 'Wheeeee!' they heard Bouncer cry breathlessly as he sailed towards Toby. But he went too high – and for a moment it looked as if he was going to plummet straight back down again.

'Oh no,' Jack murmured anxiously, positioning himself ready to catch Bouncer. Luckily, Toby had seen what was happening and, in the blink of an eye, held out a paw and managed to grab Bouncer as he fell past him.

Willow held her breath as Toby hauled
Bouncer on to the windowsill, and then
both Hoozles waved down at them to show
all was well.

'Phew,' Jack said, wiping his forehead.
'That was close.'

The two toys squeezed through the open
window and just a few moments later,

Willow and Jack could hear them trying to unlatch the front door. After a bit of scrabbling, the door swung open. They were in!

'Hello?' Willow called into the house. 'Mr Mayor, where are you? We've come to get you out!'

'I'm upstairs!' came the shouted reply. 'In the bathroom!'

Willow and Jack ran upstairs, carrying their Hoozles. On the landing they saw two rooms ahead of them. One door was open, and one had been wedged shut with a door stop. Croc must have done it!

'Just a moment,' Jack called, pulling out the door stop. He tried the handle. 'There,' he said, as the door swung open.

The Mayor came out, still in his pyjamas. 'Thank you so much,' he said. 'I've been stuck in there all morning. Can't think how on earth that happened. And now there's only minutes before the parade begins! Do excuse me, children, but I must get dressed. I'll be with you as soon as I can.'

He rushed into his bedroom and shut the door, emerging moments later in his full ceremonial robes. 'Oh dear, I was meant to be at the toy shop ages ago, wasn't I?' he said to Willow, fastening his watch. 'I'm so sorry. Did your aunt send you to track me down? I'm jolly glad she did.'

Willow smiled. 'She said she'd see you at the start of the parade, and she'd take Wizard with her,' she told the Mayor. 'If we hurry, we'll be just in time to meet her.'

'Wonderful,' the Mayor replied. 'What are we waiting for? Let's go!'

The three of them raced towards the centre of town as fast as they could. A crowd had gathered now and some people cheered the Mayor as he went by. There was a lovely, buzzy atmosphere as everyone waited for the parade to begin, and Willow felt excitement building inside her. She was so relieved that they'd found the Mayor and stopped Croc from spoiling everything!

They reached the front of the parade where the floats had been set up in preparation for the grand procession. 'We made it,' Willow sighed happily.

'Yes, we did,' the Mayor agreed, but then his smile faded. 'Wait a moment though, where's your aunt, and Wizard?' he asked.

'We can't start the parade without them!'

Willow gazed around in dismay. It was true – Auntie Suzy, Freddie and the other Hoozles were nowhere to be seen! Oh, no. Had Croc somehow got to them too?

Chapter Six

'I'll be able to see better from up here,' the
Mayor decided, climbing up on to the float
to look for Auntie Suzy.

While he was peering at the crowd,
Willow caught sight of an orange streak on
the float. 'There's Croc!' she hissed to Jack.
'What's he planning now?'

'Something else to ruin the parade, I bet,'
Jack replied. 'We've got to stop him!'

Willow was just about to jump on to
the float herself and grab the naughty

crocodile when the Mayor reached down and scooped him up. 'Ahh! So your aunt has been here after all,' the Mayor said to Willow, holding Croc. 'She must have left me this Hoozle to hold – and what a fine fellow he is, too. A wonderful substitute for Wizard. Look at his lovely smile!'

Willow nearly got the giggles, imagining how furious Croc would be to hear the Mayor praising his 'lovely smile'. The crowd cheered as the Mayor held Croc up to show them, and Willow was sure she spotted a sulky look in Croc's eyes. She knew very well that he must be hating all of this. Being cheered by happy Hoozle-loving people was not exactly Croc's idea of fun!

'Sorry we're so late!' came a panting voice just then and Willow, Jack and the Mayor turned to see Auntie Suzy and Freddie running over. Auntie Suzy's hair was tumbling out of its ponytail and she was red in the face, but she was carrying all three members of the Hoozle Council, and Freddie had Wobbly on his shoulders too. 'We waited until the very last minute to

leave,' Auntie Suzy explained. 'Just in case you showed up at the toy shop.'

The Mayor didn't seem to hear Auntie Suzy very clearly over the noise of the excited crowd. He beamed at her and held up Croc. 'Not to worry, my dear, we found the Hoozle you left for me,' he said. 'Very nice little chap, this. Extra cuddly!'

Willow didn't dare meet Jack's eye for fear of bursting out laughing. And if she wasn't mistaken she was sure she'd heard a tiny growl of rage escaping from Croc!

Auntie Suzy looked from Croc to Willow, her eyes puzzled. Willow tried to indicate with a smile that it was all OK, and just part of a Hoozle adventure. Auntie Suzy knew all about the magic qualities of the Hoozles, of course, so she just smiled politely at the Mayor and said she was glad he liked Croc.

'Now then, we'd better get this show on the road,' the Mayor said. 'And I'd like my two rescuers to come and stand with me, please.' He held out a hand for first Willow and then Jack to climb up on the float with their Hoozles. 'You two saved the day,' he told them. 'Thank goodness you found me!' Then he turned to the crowd. 'Are we all ready? Then let the Summertown Spectacular parade . . . BEGIN!'

A huge cheer went up as the Mayor pressed a button and the float began to move slowly along the road. Auntie Suzy and Freddie walked beside them, holding Wizard, Lovely, Grouchy and Wobbly. To Willow's delight, she noticed that lots of people in the crowd were holding their own Hoozles too – a green zebra Hoozle, a pink hippo Hoozle, a black cat Hoozle with a long velvety tail, and many more. How

lovely to think that there were so many Hoozles living happily in Summertown!

Willow looked across at Jack with a big smile on her face, and made Toby wave his arm at Jack and Bouncer. Jack grinned back at Willow as he made Bouncer wave too. Now they both knew the special secret about the Hoozles. What fun, thought Willow with a rush of excitement. She couldn't wait to find out what Hoozle adventures they would have together!

They're not just toys –
they're the magical hoozles!
And every Hoozle needs
a special friend . . .

Collect all these wonderful Hoozle stories!

Book 1: My Magical Teddy

When Willow and
Freddie go to stay at
Auntie Suzy's toyshop by
the sea they're in for the
adventure of a lifetime
with the wonderful
magical Hoozles.
Freddie's Hoozle needs
help and it's up to
Willow and her new pals
to come to the rescue.

Book 2: The Naughty Croc

When lonely Jack comes to Auntie Suzy's toyshop, Willow and Freddie know just what he needs – a magical Hoozle! But soon Croc the naughty Hoozle is out causing trouble for everyone. Can they stop his mean plans and find Jack the perfect cuddly friend?

Book 3: A Penguin Problem

Grouchy the penguin Hoozle is feeling poorly, and naughty Croc is causing mischief and mayhem all over Summertown. Can Willow and her Hoozle friends help Grouchy get better and spoil Croc's fiendish plans all at once?